Teen Choices Workbook

Facilitator Reproducible Self-Assessments, Exercises & Educational Handouts

John J. Liptak, EdD
Ester A. Leutenberg

Illustrated by
Amy L. Brodsky, LISW-S

Duluth, Minnesota

Whole Person
101 West 2nd St., Suite 203
Duluth, MN 55802

800-247-6789

books@wholeperson.com
www.wholeperson.com

Teen Choices Workbook
Facilitator Reproducible Self-Assessments,
Exercises & Educational Handouts

Copyright ©2011 by Ester A. Leutenberg and John J. Liptak.
All rights reserved. Except for short excerpts for review purposes and materials in the assessment, journaling activities, and educational handouts sections, no part of this book may be reproduced or transmitted in any form by any means, electronic or mechanical without permission in writing from the publisher. Self-assessments, exercises, and educational handouts are meant to be photocopied.

All efforts have been made to ensure accuracy of the information contained in this book as of the date published. The author(s) and the publisher expressly disclaim responsibility for any adverse effects arising from the use or application of the information contained herein.

Printed in the United States of America

10 9 8 7 6 5 4 3 2 1

Editorial Director: Carlene Sippola
Art Director: Joy Morgan Dey

Library of Congress Control Number: 2011927796
ISBN: 978-1-57025-255-6

Using This Book (For the professional)

Life is about making choices. Today's teens live in a far more challenging atmosphere than past generations and they face many important choices that both positively and negatively affect their growth and development. Their success in life is a result of the choices they make as they mature and that they will make in the future.

Choices come in many different forms. Decisions must be made for a wide variety of options:
- *Should I be friends with her?*
- *What should I do if I am offered a cigarette?*
- *Should I go to a party where I know there will be alcohol and drugs?*
- *Should I socialize with people about whom I have an iffy feeling?*
- *Should I engage in extreme sports?*
- *Should I join the French Club in school?*
- *Should I study business or journalism?*
- *Should I go on vacation with my family or stay home with my friends?*
- *What should I do if my friends want me to try illegal drugs?*
- *Should I drop out of school?*
- *Should I be intimate with my boyfriend or girlfriend?*
- *Should I apply for college?*
- *Should I join a gang?*

These can be very difficult questions for teens to answers as they begin to test their boundaries, explore individual autonomy, and begin making decisions for themselves. To help teens become more thoughtful decision-makers, *Teen Choices Workbook* will guide them to act responsibly, reflect on decisions they have made in the past, explore the consequences of those decisions, and take responsibility for future decisions. These reflections and discussions will guide them to be better decision-makers, as well as to confirm their positive past decisions.

During adolescence, making effective independent choices is often a point of contention between teens and adults (parents, teachers, grandparents, etc.). As teens mature, they face increasing demands to learn to make choices more independently and to take more responsibility for their own choices. Choices allow teens to change how they are currently living their lives (if they are not happy where they are) or continue to live responsibly by making even more effective choices.

(Continued on the next page)

Using This Book *(For the professional, continued)*

The *Teen Choices Workbook* is designed to help teens engage in self-reflection, examine personal thoughts and feelings that go into the decisions they have made, and learn valuable tools and techniques for making effective decisions in the future. This book combines three powerful psychological tools for the management of thoughts, feelings, and behaviors: self-assessment and journaling. Role-playing exercises are a third component to enhance empathy and allow adolescents to practice decision-making strategies.

The *Teen Choices Workbook* contains five separate sections to help participants learn more about choices they have made and choices they have yet to make in their lives:

- **Teen Action Choices Scale** helps teens analyze the factors that primarily influence the decisions they make and define how effectively they are using their time.
- **Teen Relationship Choices Scale** helps teens examine how they make choices about acquaintances, friends, best friends and dating friends.
- **Teen Cultural Differences Scale** helps teens explore how accepting and receptive they are to people who are different from themselves.
- **Teen "Not-So-Great" Choices Scale** helps teens reconsider the choices they made in the past that were not successful and outline more effective decision-making techniques.
- **Teen Risk-Taking Behavior Scale** helps teens investigate both the positive and the negative risks they have taken and discover ways to choose healthy risks.

Use Codes for Confidentiality

Confidentiality is a term for any action that preserves the privacy of other people. Because teens completing the activities in this workbook might be asked to answer assessment items and to journal about and explore their relationships, you will need to discuss confidentiality before you begin using the materials in this workbook. Maintaining confidentiality is important because it shows respect for others and allows participants to explore their feelings without hurting anyone's feelings or fearing gossip, harm or retribution.

In order to maintain confidentiality, explain to the participants that they need to assign a **name code for each person or each group of people** they write about as they complete the various activities in the workbook. For example, a friend named Joey who enjoys going to hockey games might be titled JLHG (Joey Loves Hockey Games) for a particular exercise. In order to protect their friends' identities, they should not use people's or groups' actual names or initials, just name codes.

(Continued on the next page)

Layout of the Book

The *Teen Choices Workbook* is designed to be used either independently or as part of an integrated curriculum. You may administer one of the assessments and the journaling exercises to an individual or a group with whom you are working, or you may administer a number of the assessments over one or more days.

This book includes the following reproducible pages in the first five sections:

- **Assessment Instruments** – Self-assessment inventories with scoring directions and interpretation materials. Group facilitators can choose one or more of the activities relevant to their participants.
- **Activity Handouts** – Practical questions and activities that prompt self-reflection and promote self-understanding. These questions and activities foster introspection and promote pro-social behaviors.
- **Quotations** – Quotations are used in each section to provide insight and promote reflection. Participants will be asked to select one or more of the quotations and journal about what the quotations mean to them.
- **Reflective Questions for Journaling** – Self-exploration activities and journaling exercises specific to each assessment to enhance self-discovery, learning, and healing.
- **Educational Handouts** – Handouts designed to enhance instruction can be used by individuals or in groups to promote a positive understanding of past choices participants have made and positive decision-making in the future. They can be distributed, scanned and converted into masters for overheads or transparencies, projected or written on boards and/or discussed.

Who Should Use This Program?

This book has been designed as a practical tool to help professionals such as therapists, counselors, psychologists, teachers, group leaders, etc. Depending on the role of the professional using the *Teen Choices Workbook* and the specific group's needs, these sections can be used individually or combined for a more comprehensive approach.

Why Use Self-Assessments?

Self-assessments are important in teaching various anger management skills because they help participants to engage in these ways:

- Become aware of the primary motivators that guide their behavior.
- Explore and learn to "let go" of troublesome habits and behavioral patterns learned in childhood.
- Examine the effects of unconscious childhood messages.
- Gain insight and "a wake-up call" for behavioral change.
- Focus thinking on behavioral goals for change.
- Uncover personal resources that can help them to cope better with problems and difficulties.
- Explore personal characteristics without judgment.
- Identify personal strengths and weaknesses.

Because the assessments are presented in a straightforward and easy-to-use format, individuals can self-administer, score and interpret each assessment at their own pace.

About the Assessments, Journaling Activities and Educational Handouts

Materials in the Assessments, Journaling Activities, and Educational Handouts sections in this book are reproducible and can be photocopied for participants' use. Assessments contained in this book focus on self-reported data and thus are similar to ones used by psychologists, counselors, therapists and career consultants. The accuracy and usefulness of the information provided is dependent on the truthful information that each participant provides. By being honest, participants help themselves to learn about unproductive and ineffective patterns in their lives, and to uncover information that might be keeping them from being as happy or as successful as they might be.

An assessment instrument can provide participants with valuable information about themselves; however, these assessments cannot measure or identify everything. The assessments' purpose is not to pigeonhole certain characteristics, but rather to allow participants to consider all of their characteristics. This book contains self-assessments, not tests. Tests measure knowledge or whether something is right or wrong. For the assessments in this book, there are no right or wrong answers. These assessments ask for personal opinions or attitudes about a topic of importance in the participant's life.

When administering the assessments in this workbook, remember that the items are generically written so that they will be applicable to a wide variety of people but will not account for every possible variable for every person. No assessments are specifically tailored to one person. Assessments are structured to help a variety of participants to identify negative themes in their lives and find ways to break the hold of these patterns and their effects.

Advise teen participants taking the assessments that they should not spend too much time trying to analyze the content of the questions; they should think about the questions in general and then spontaneously report how they feel about each one. Whatever the results of the assessment, encourage participants to talk about their findings and their feelings pertaining to what have they discovered about themselves. Talking about issues such as aggression and bullying can be therapeutic and beneficial.

The *Teen Choices Workbook* sections serve as an avenue for individual self-reflection, as well as group experiences revolving around identified topics of importance. Each assessment includes directions for easy administration, scoring and interpretation. In addition, each section includes exploratory activities, reflective journaling activities, insightful quotations and educational handouts to help participants to learn more about the choices they have made, explore their habitual, ineffective methods of making choices, and define new ways for choosing more effective life options.

(Continued on the next page)

About the Assessments, Journaling Activities and Educational Handouts *(continued)*

The art of self-reflection goes back many centuries and is rooted in many of the world's greatest spiritual and philosophical traditions. Socrates, the ancient Greek philosopher, was known to walk the streets engaging the people he met in philosophical reflection and dialogue. He felt that this type of activity was so important in life that he proclaimed, "The unexamined life is not worth living!" The unexamined life is one in which the same routine is continually repeated without ever thinking about its meaning to one's life and how this life really could be lived. However, a structured reflection and examination of beliefs, assumptions, characteristics and patterns can provide a better understanding which can lead to a more satisfying life and career. A greater level of self-understanding about important life skills is often necessary to make positive, self-directed changes in repetitive negative patterns throughout life. The assessments and exercises in this book can help promote this self-understanding. Through involvement with the in-depth activities, each participant claims ownership in the development of positive patterns.

Journaling is an extremely powerful tool for enhancing self-discovery, learning, transcending traditional problems, breaking ineffective life and career habits, and helping people to heal from psychological traumas of the past. From a physical point of view, writing reduces stress and lowers muscle tension, blood pressure and heart rate levels. Psychologically, writing reduces feelings of sadness, depression and general anxiety, and it leads to a greater level of life satisfaction and optimism. Behaviorally, writing leads to enhanced social skills, emotional intelligence and creativity.

By combining reflective assessment and journaling, your participants will engage in a powerful method for helping teens make more effective life choices.

Thanks to the following professionals whose input in this book has been invaluable!

Amy Brodsky, LISW-S

Carol Butler, MS Ed, RN, C

Kathy Khalsa, MAJS, OTR/L

Jay Leutenberg

Kathy Liptak, Ed.D.

Eileen Regen, M.Ed., CJE

For the Facilitator:

Enrichment Activities for Each Section

by Carol Butler, MS, Ed, RN,C

These options provide interaction and enjoyment for the teens. They can be used as you present a new section, or as a conclusion after participants finish the written exercises.

TEEN ACTION CHOICES

1. Collages

- Provide magazines, scissors, glue, and paper or poster board.
- Ask each participant to make a collage showing personal preferences of material possessions and activities.
- Participants show their work, share their "likes" and receive peer feedback.
- List these categories on the board or on a large paper: Creativity, Fitness, Science, Helping, Family, Leadership, Mechanical/Technical and/or Nature.
- Peers identify predominant themes in each other's collages.

2. What Would You Do?

- List these roles on the board or on a large paper:
  Student, Employee, Child, Friend, Volunteer.
- Ask a participant to read this scenario:

  "You have an unexpected day off from school and work. You have a school project due in two days. Your boss asks you to work an extra shift and you really need the money. Your parents want you to babysit your younger siblings. Your friends invite you to a barbeque which a prospective dating friend will be attending. The library where you volunteer desperately needs your help. What would you do?"

- The participant (reader) encourages peers to share what they would do, why, which role is most important to them, and how they would compromise or combine roles.
- Examples: Take the young siblings to select books while doing volunteer work at the library in the morning; attend the barbeque in the evening, etc.

(Continued on the next page)

Enrichment Activities for Each Section

TEEN RELATIONSHIP CHOICES

Role plays

Place two chairs facing each other in the front of the group and ask volunteers to practice these scenerios:

- Starting a conversation based on mutual interests, and discussing things in common.

- Asking open-ended questions, then paraphrasing and reflecting the responder's thoughts/feelings.

TEEN CULTURAL DIFFERENCES

What Would You Do?

- Ask volunteers to take turns reading the scenarios below. Elicit peer feedback.

    "You are at the lunch table with your friends. A person who is mentally ill or developmentally disabled sits next to you. Your friends move away slightly and ignore the person. What would you do?"

    "A lonely elderly neighbor starts a conversation with you almost every time you walk outside. You are usually in a hurry. What would you do?"

    "You really hit it off with a classmate of another race with whom you have many common interests. Your family will not allow that person in your house and forbid you to go places with him/her. What would you do?"

(Continued on the next page)

Enrichment Activities for Each Section

(Page 3 of 4)

TEEN "NOT-SO-GREAT" CHOICES

1. **Dramatization/Scenario:** Photocopy the following script. Give each of three volunteer actors a copy of the script. Provide cell phones. Allow the three "actors" to practice a couple of times before the skit. Tell the group they are going to see a skit and will be asked questions afterward.

    > **Narrator:** *Jane and Bill have been sitting next to each other in math class, and she has been hoping he would ask her out. Yesterday she was thrilled when he asked for her phone number.*
    >
    > **Bill:** *Dials a number and Jane answers.*
    >
    > **Jane:** *Hello.*
    >
    > **Bill:** *Hey, how are you? This is Bill from math class.*
    >
    > **Jane:** *Doin' fine.*
    >
    > **Bill:** *I was wondering if you'd like to hang out on Saturday. Maybe we could go to a movie or to an amusement park?*
    >
    > **Jane:** *I'd love to!*
    >
    > **Narrator:** *They went out and had a great time. Jane told her friends the details.*
    >
    > **Jane:** *I think we have a chance of seeing each other more and dating.*
    >
    > **Narrator:** *Monday at school, Bill is in class with Jane. After class he approaches her.*
    >
    > **Bill:** *I really had a good time with you and hope we can get together again.*
    >
    > **Jane:** *Me too.*
    >
    > **Narrator:** *That night he calls Jane.*
    >
    > **Bill:** *Hey Jane, I have a little favor to ask. Since we sit next to each other, during tomorrow's math test, do you think you could let me see your answers? You are so much better in math than I am, and I really need your help.*
    >
    > **Narrator:** *What are Jane's options?*

    Then . . .
    - Peers share and discuss their opinions.
    - Facilitator lists on board or large paper – Critical Thinking, Impulsivity, Peer Pressure, Independence – and asks participants to discuss Jane's possible thoughts/actions regarding critical thinking, impulsivity, peer pressure and/or independence.

2. **Real Life:** Ask participants to share situations they have experienced or may face. Select one that lends itself to the steps below, summarize it on the board or large paper and list these items:
    - Identify the decision to be made.
    - Identify the potential choices.
    - Identify and compare all possible consequences
    - Make a decision based on the information available.
    - Act and evaluate the results

Encourage participants to discuss the above steps related to the summarized situation.

(Continued on the next page)

Enrichment Activities for Each Section

TEEN RISK-TAKING

Brainstorming

- List on board or large paper the following categories:
  School, Social, Activities, Family, Friends, Substances, Physical, Criminal, Health.
- Divide the participants into partners or small groups and provide them with one piece of paper and pen per partnership or small group.
- Ask each partnership or small group to select one or a few of the above categories
- Ask each partnership or small group to list at least two positive and two negative risks for each of their selected categories.
- The whole group re-convenes and the partners or small group members take turns going to the front of the room.
- A spokesperson shares their examples and receives feedback from others.
- Note that something that seems to have only negative risks such as "Criminal" can have positive risks. *Example: A friend is shop-lifting.* **Positive risk** – *Leave the store immediately without the person and risk losing the friendship;* **Negative risk** – *Stay with the person and risk getting caught.*

Cut ups

- Photocopy and cut out each phrase below:

Bad Feelings About self	Wanting/Needing Acceptance
Little or No Confidence	Wanting/Needing Popularity
Peer Pressure	Thrill-Seeking
Loneliness	Fear of Family/Friends' Reactions

- Place the folded cut-ups in a cup or envelope.
- Pass the cup.
- Participants take turns reading the slip of paper they picked and identifying an associated positive and negative risk.
- Peers give feedback and add more positive and negative risks if possible.

Introduction for the Participant

Beginning right now, and into the future, you will make many significant choices that will affect your life greatly. Choices can have positive and/or negative consequences. Each choice will require careful thought and wise decision-making. As you have grown from childhood into your young adult years, you are expected to be increasingly responsible for the choices you make. The choices you have made have influenced your life, and the choices you will make in the future will largely determine the direction your life.

Many of your choices will be based on a logical decision-making process related to these factors:

Relationships Choices – You will be making choices about people. Who should you choose as an acquaintance, friend, best friend and person to date?

Behaving Toward Others – You will be making choices about how you treat other people, some just like you and others who are different from you.

Time Choices – You will be making choices about how to use your time most effectively and efficiently.

Risks – You will be making choices about the consequences of taking both positive and negative risks in your life.

The *Teen Choices Workbook* is designed to help you learn more about how you have made decisions in the past, and explore ways of making future decisions.

You will be asked to respond to assessments and exercises and to journal about some experiences in your relationships. Everyone has the right to confidentiality, and you need to honor the right of their privacy. Think about it this way – you would not want someone writing things about you that other people could read. Your friends feel this way also.

In order to maintain the confidentiality of your friends, assign code names to people or groups, based on things you know about them. For example, a friend named Sherry who loves to wear purple might be coded as SWP (Sherry Wears Purple). **Do not use any person's or groups' actual name when you are listing people or groups of people – Use only name codes.**

Teen Choices Workbook
TABLE OF CONTENTS

SECTION I – Teen Action Choices Scale

    Directions 19
    Teen Action Choices Scale 20–23
    Scoring Directions 24
    Profile Interpretation 24
    Scale Descriptions 25–27

Exercises

    My Activity Time 28
    Activities I Enjoy and Might Enjoy 29

Journaling Activities

    How I Spend My Time 30–31
    Making Effective Time Choices 32–33
    Each Week 34
    You Can Do It! 35
    Making Wise Choices Quotes 36

Educational Handouts

    Teens and Time Management 37

SECTION II – Teen Relationship Choices Scale

    Directions 41
    Teen Relationship Choices Scale 42–43
    Scoring Directions 44
    Profile Interpretation 44
    Scale Descriptions and Exercises
        Secure 45
        Anxious 46
        Independent 47

Exercises

    Acquaintances 48
    Getting to Know You 49
    My Friends 50
    Developing Positive Relationships 51
    Ending Negative Relationships 51

TABLE OF CONTENTS

    Best Friends 52

    Being a Better Friend 53

    Dating Friends 54

Journaling Activities

    Relationship Quotations. 55

    Journaling About Relationships 56–57

Educational Handouts

    Developing New Relationships 58

    Nurturing Long-Lasting Relationships 59

SECTION III – Teen Cultural Differences Scale

    Directions 63

    Teen Cultural Differences Scale 64–65

    Scoring Directions 66

    Profile Interpretation 66

    Profile Descriptions 67

Exercises

    Valuing Diversity 68

    Interact with Diverse Individuals 69

    Your Own Cultural Identity 70

    Avoid Stereotyping 71

    My Stereotypes 72–73

    People from Other Countries 74

    People with a Different Sexual Orientation 75

    People with Special Needs or Health Issues 76

    People from a Different Race or Religion 77

    People in a Different Financial Situation. 78

Journaling Activities

    What I Learned about Myself 79

Educational Handouts

    The Cycle of Hatred. 80

Journaling Activities

    The Cycle of Hatred Quotations. 81

TABLE OF CONTENTS

SECTION IV – Teen "not-so-great" Choices Scale

    Directions 85
    Teen "Not-So-Great" Choices Scale 86
    Scoring Directions 87
    Profile Interpretation 88
    Scale Descriptions 89

Exercises

    Past "Not-So-Great" Choices 90
    Critical Thinking 91
    A Logical Decision-Making Process 92–93
    Impulsive Behavior 94
    Peer Pressure 95
    Peer Pressure in Your Life 96
    Independent Status 97
    Your Independent Status 98

Journaling Activities

    Critical Thinking 99
    Peer Pressure 100
    Choice Quotations 101

Educational Handouts

    Important Decisions 102
    Questions to Ask When Facing a Decision 103

SECTION V – Teen Risk-Taking Scale

    Teen Positive and Negative Risk-Taking Scales Directions . . . 107
Teen Positive Risk-Taking Scale 108
    Teen Positive Risk-Taking Scale Scoring Directions 109
    Teen Positive Risk-Taking Scale Profile Interpretation 109

Exercises

    Positive Risks at School 110
    Positive Risks in My Social Life 111
    Positive Risks in My Activities 112

TABLE OF CONTENTS

    Positive Risks with My Family and Friends. 113
    Positive Risks in the Future 114

Teen Negative Risk-Taking Scale 115
    Teen Negative Risk-Taking Scale Scoring Directions. 116
    Teen Negative Risk-Taking Scale Profile Interpretation. 116

Exercises
    Negative Risks with Substances. 117
    Negative Physical Risks 118
    Negative Criminal Risks 119
    Negative Health Risks 120
    Learning about Negative Risks. 121

Journaling Activities
    Motivations 122
    Risk-Taking Quotations 123

Educational Handouts
    Positive Risk-Taking. 124
    Negative Risk-Taking 125

SECTION I:
Teen Action Choices Scale

Name_____

Date_____

SECTION I: TEEN ACTION CHOICES SCALE

Teen Action Choices Scale Directions

An important aspect of developing and growing as a teen is making appropriate action choices on how to spend your time. Your time might involve activities such as hobbies, school, friends, recreation, family, work, volunteering, crafts, music, sports and clubs.

This scale will help you identify your primary interests and perhaps inspire some new ideas. Read each statement carefully. Circle the number of the response that shows how descriptive each statement is of you. Please answer all the questions to the best of your ability using the following scale:

4 = Always or **A Great Deal**

3 = Often or **Quite a Lot**

2 = Sometimes or **Some**

1 = Rarely, if Ever

I enjoy . . .

1. dancing 4   ③   2   1

In the above example, the circled 3 indicates that the test taker often likes to dance or watch other people dance.

This is not a test and there are no right or wrong answers. Do not spend too much time thinking about your answers. Your initial response will be most true for you. Be sure to respond to every statement.

(Turn to the next page and begin)

SECTION I: TEEN ACTION CHOICES SCALE

Teen Action Choices Scale

Please respond to each of the statements by circling the response which best describes you:

4 = Always
or
A Great Deal

3 = Often
or
Quite a Lot

2 = Sometimes
or
Some

**1 = Rarely,
if Ever**

I enjoy . . .

1. dancing 4   3   2   1

2. drawing, painting, or sculpting 4   3   2   1

3. writing poetry, stories, etc. 4   3   2   1

4. playing an instrument 4   3   2   1

5. singing 4   3   2   1

6. attending plays or musicals 4   3   2   1

7. crafts of any kind (sewing, making models, etc.) 4   3   2   1

TOTAL - C = _____

I enjoy . . .

8. activities that keep me fit and trim 4   3   2   1

9. training for marathons and athletic events 4   3   2   1

10. exercises to get or stay in shape 4   3   2   1

11. learning and practicing healthy nutrition 4   3   2   1

12. taking aerobics and fitness classes 4   3   2   1

13. weightlifting or martial arts 4   3   2   1

14. playing sports 4   3   2   1

TOTAL - F1 = _____

(Continued on the next page)

SECTION I: TEEN ACTION CHOICES SCALE

(Teen Action Choices Scale continued)

Please respond to each of the statements by circling the response which best describes you:

4 = Always
or
A Great Deal

3 = Often
or
Quite a Lot

2 = Sometimes
or
Some

**1 = Rarely,
if Ever**

I enjoy . . .

15. reading about science	4	3	2	1
16. looking through a microscope	4	3	2	1
17. visiting museums and/or historical sites	4	3	2	1
18. working mathematical games	4	3	2	1
19. doing science experiments	4	3	2	1
20. watching scientific television shows	4	3	2	1
21. participating in science fairs	4	3	2	1

TOTAL - S = _____

I enjoy . . .

22. helping other people	4	3	2	1
23. volunteering in the community	4	3	2	1
24. supporting friends with personal problems	4	3	2	1
25. teaching things to others	4	3	2	1
26. being with children	4	3	2	1
27. interacting with people from other cultures	4	3	2	1
28. tutoring others in school	4	3	2	1

TOTAL - H = _____

(Continued on the next page)

SECTION I: TEEN ACTION CHOICES SCALE

(Teen Action Choices Scale continued)

Please respond to each of the statements by circling the response which best describes you:

4 = Always	**3 = Often**	**2 = Sometimes**	**1 = Rarely,**
or	or	or	if Ever
A Great Deal	**Quite a Lot**	**Some**	

I enjoy . . .

29. talking with my family	4	3	2	1
30. helping around the house (baking, yard work, etc.)	4	3	2	1
31. having friends spend time with my family	4	3	2	1
32. spending evenings at home with my family	4	3	2	1
33. caring for my family	4	3	2	1
34. vacationing with my family	4	3	2	1
35. playing board, card and computer games with family	4	3	2	1

TOTAL - F2 = _____

I enjoy . . .

36. coordinating family, neighborhood and/or school events	4	3	2	1
37. being a leader in school clubs and organizations	4	3	2	1
38. organizing group activities	4	3	2	1
39. making decisions	4	3	2	1
40. working with money	4	3	2	1
41. being responsible	4	3	2	1
42. planning activities for others	4	3	2	1

TOTAL - L = _____

(Continued on the next page)

SECTION I: TEEN ACTION CHOICES SCALE

(Teen Action Choices Scale continued)

Please respond to each of the statements by circling the response which best describes you:

4 = Always
or
A Great Deal

3 = Often
or
Quite a Lot

2 = Sometimes
or
Some

1 = Rarely, if Ever

I enjoy . . .

43. playing high tech games	4	3	2	1
44. using hand tools	4	3	2	1
45. helping people with their computers	4	3	2	1
46. working on and repairing cars	4	3	2	1
47. writing computer programs	4	3	2	1
48. tinkering with engines	4	3	2	1
49. researching what makes things work	4	3	2	1

TOTAL - M/T = _____

I enjoy . . .

50. playing with animals	4	3	2	1
51. walking, running, hiking, exercising outdoors	4	3	2	1
52. raising plants and flowers	4	3	2	1
53. volunteering in an animal shelter	4	3	2	1
54. cutting grass and caring for lawns	4	3	2	1
55. gardening	4	3	2	1
56. spending time in parks	4	3	2	1

TOTAL - N = _____

(Go to the Scoring Directions on the next page)

SECTION I: TEEN ACTION CHOICES SCALE

Teen Action Choices Scale
Scoring Directions

The scale you have just completed will help you identify various types of activities that you are already enjoying and some you may have not considered until now. It is designed to measure your interests and help you identify activities related to your interests. For each of the sections on the previous pages, count the scores you circled for each of the sections. Put that total on the line marked TOTAL at the end of each section.

Then, transfer your totals to the spaces below:

TOTALS

C   = Creative Scale   _____   F2   = Family Scale   _____

F1   = Fitness Scale   _____   L   = Leadership Scale   _____

S   = Science Scale   _____   M/T = Mechanical/Technical Scale _____

H   = Helping Scale   _____   N   = Nature Scale   _____

After you have completed transferring your total scores, you should look at the Profile Interpretation section for more information about your scores on the assessment.

Profile Interpretation

Individual Scale Score	Result	Indications
7 to 13	low	You are probably not interested in the types of activities in this scale.
14 to 21	moderate	You probably have some interest in the types of activities in this scale.
22 to 28	high	You are probably very interested in the types of activities in this scale.

SECTION I: TEEN ACTION CHOICES SCALE

Teen Action Choices – Scale Descriptions

1. Creative

If you scored high on this scale you are probably interested in creatively expressing yourself through artistic endeavors. You benefit by expressing your feelings and ideas in creative ways. Finding activities that tap into your specific talents will allow creative expression.

Since you enjoy creativity you might consider such activities as painting, drawing, sketching, sculpting, photography, writing poems, ceramics, writing short stories, pottery, origami, reading, needlework, crafts, attending arts festivals, acting in school plays and/or community theatre, blogging, scrapbooking, designing web pages, taking dance lessons, or singing in a choir.

You might consider such occupations as photographer, author, journalist, designer (graphic, fashion or interior), sound engineer, curator or desktop publisher.

2. Fitness

If you scored high on this scale you are probably interested in physically challenging activities that help to keep you physically fit. Participating in physical activities is a powerful way for you to reduce your tension and anxiety.

Since you enjoy fitness you might consider such activities as tennis, marathons, darts, martial arts, chopping wood, yoga, mountain climbing, kayaking, scuba diving, climbing walls, coaching children's athletic games, amateur sports, weight lifting, health clubs, exercising, jogging, aerobics, softball, yoga, skiing, bowling, swimming, traveling, cycling, mall walking, or canoeing.

You might consider such occupations as athletic trainer, nurse, physician, health educator, physicians assistant, nutritionist, physical, speech, occupational or massage therapist.

3. Science

If you scored high on this scale you are probably interested in discovering, collecting, and analyzing information about the natural world, life sciences and human behavior.

Since you enjoy science you might consider such leisure activities as astronomy, science fairs, health care volunteer, building model rockets, mathematical puzzles, amateur archeology, meteorology, star gazing, collecting rocks, exploring caves, weather watching, reading about technological developments, visiting planetariums and science museums, computer games, studying anatomy, prospecting, conducting experiments with plants, doing chemistry experiments, or watching aerospace shows on television.

You might consider such occupations as engineer, biologist, sociologist, zoologist, geologist, historian, geographer, computer software engineer, science journalist, educator or biochemist.

(continued on the next page)

SECTION I: TEEN ACTION CHOICES SCALE

Teen Action Choices – Scale Descriptions (continued)

4. Helping

If you scored high on this scale you are probably interested in improving people's social, mental, emotional and spiritual well-being. You feel a desire to give back to other people and you like to feel that you are making a difference in others' lives.

Since you enjoy helping, you might consider volunteering your time to help others in such activities as tutoring, volunteering with the elderly and/or disabled, or helping in a hospital, working with church groups, volunteering to work at a homeless shelter, babysitting, caring for children, visiting friends, planning events, entertaining, serving as a mental health volunteer, or teaching English as a second language.

> **You might consider such occupations** as teacher, social worker, occupational, physical, speech or massage therapist, counselor, psychologist, police officer, child care worker, protective service worker, probation officer or community service manager/planner.

5. Family

If you scored high on this scale you are probably interested in activities which allow you to spend quality time with members of your family.

Since you enjoy being with your family and/or extended family, you might consider such activities as baking pastries, cake decorating, hosting parties, sewing, cooking, cutting hair for family members, planning family recreational activities, traveling with family members, shopping, going to school athletic events or concerts, watching sports, handling equipment for a local athletic team, preparing and serving meals at a food kitchen, teaching others how to cook or bake, canning and preserving food, or cooking for community events.

> **You might consider such occupations** as cook, chef, manicurist, recreation worker, recreation or family therapist, tour guide, travel agent, sports official, baker, cosmetologist, food preparation manager or personal care worker.

6. Leadership

If you scored high on this scale you are probably interested in being in charge and coordinating events. Alan Keith of Genentech states, "Leadership is ultimately about creating a way for people to contribute to making something extraordinary happen."

Since you enjoy being a leader, you might consider such activities such as being an officer or on the board in a school, your community or local charitable organization; coaching; organizing neighborhood activities and coordinating community events; holding office in school; fund raising; serving on the urban planning committee; or as a scout leader; studying financial trends and organizing a teen investment group with an adult supervisor; participating in spiritual or religious events or political campaigns; coordinating a camping trip; or organizing family activities.

> **You might consider such occupations** as an owner or manager of a business, charity or foundation, auditor, salesperson, administrative assistant, budget analyst, billing clerk, human resources manager, financial planner, marketing representative, personnel recruiter, payroll clerk, school board member or a politician.

(Continued on the next page)

SECTION I: TEEN ACTION CHOICES SCALE

Teen Action Choices – Scale Descriptions (continued)

7. Mechanical/Technical

If you scored high on this scale you are probably interested in learning about and understanding how things work. You are probably good at visualizing and solving mechanical problems, working with your hands and with tools, and using, creating and troubleshooting technology.

Since you enjoy mechanical activities you might consider such activities as fixing appliances, repairing computers, woodworking, painting and home repairs, repairing cars, wood carving and metal work, building cabinets, refurbishing antiques, plumbing, working on heating and air conditioners, reading blueprints, building houses for Habitat for Humanity, rebuilding old cars.

You might consider such occupations as an automobile mechanic, air traffic controller, brick mason, electrician, building inspector, engineer, draftsman, construction manager, machine designer or operator, carpet installer, heating and air conditioner mechanic, or surveyor.

Since you enjoy the technological field you might consider such activities as creating video games or Websites, reading about developments in technology, repairing computers, giving computer lessons, researching new advancements in technology, or creating a new computer program for a school class.

You might consider such occupations as a computer programmer, software developer, systems analyst, database administrator, security specialist, graphic designer, network and computer systems administrator, employer or employee of a computer-based business.

8. Nature

If you scored high on this scale you are probably interested in animals, birds or plants, being outdoors, getting your hands dirty, and working with and being tuned into nature. Nature refers to the phenomena of the physical world. You possibly feel a spiritual connection when you are outdoors in a beautiful natural setting.

Since you enjoy nature, you might consider such activities as bird watching, riding horses, owning, playing or showing dogs, grooming animals, farming, learning about plants, going on hikes, taking nature walks, fishing, camping, visiting state parks, flower arranging, pet boarding, growing house plants, gardening, owning and/or playing with pets, or landscaping. Another option is volunteering in a veterinarian's office, animal shelter, nature museum or park.

You might consider such occupations as animal breeder, fish and game warden, forester, conservation worker, park naturalist or docent, veterinarian, zoologist, wildlife biologist, environmentalist, pest control worker, outdoor educator, hiking leader or florist.

© 2011 WHOLE PERSON ASSOCIATES, 101 WEST 2ND ST., SUITE 203, DULUTH MN 55802 • 800-247-6789

SECTION I: ACTIVITY HANDOUTS

My Activity Time

Young adults make many choices daily about how to spend their time. Considering and choosing how to spend that time effectively is the challenge. Most teens spend a substantial amount of their day in school and doing school work. They also have other responsibilities and still want some time to have fun. Making effective choices about how to spend your time is critical. In the following table describe how you spend your time in each area of your life during a typical week. Then assign an estimated per cent of the time that you spend in the activity areas.

Activity Areas	Activities I Engage in Each Week	%
Ex: Computer, etc.	*Email, Facebook, Twitter, Cell phone, Text, etc.*	*40%*
Computer, cell phones, technological objects		
Working and/or volunteering		
Clubs, house of worship, community groups		
Family/home obligations		
Fun/leisure time activities		
Other responsibilities		

SECTION I: ACTIVITY HANDOUTS

Activities I Enjoy or Might Enjoy

Now look at your results on the assessment you just completed. In the first column, list your three highest interest areas. Then, identify some leisure activities, volunteer opportunities, and occupations of interest to you. In the "Other" block, feel free to list activities and occupations from other interest areas.

Interest Areas	Activities I Like or Might Like
Interest Area #1 _____	Leisure Activities _____ Volunteer _____ Occupations _____
Interest Area #2 _____	Leisure Activities _____ Volunteer _____ Occupations _____
Interest Area #3 _____	Leisure Activities _____ Volunteer _____ Occupations _____
Interest Area #4 _____	Leisure Activities _____ Volunteer _____ Occupations _____

© 2011 WHOLE PERSON ASSOCIATES, 101 WEST 2ND ST., SUITE 203, DULUTH MN 55802 ▪ 800-247-6789

SECTION I: JOURNALING ACTIVITIES

How I Spend My Time

Teens are also called upon to make choices about how to spend their time effectively. Most teens spend a lot of time in school and with school-related activities. However, you also spend your time in fun activities, civic responsibilities and work. Making effective choices about how to spend your time is critical. In the following table describe how you spend your time in each area during a typical week.

Then assign an estimated per cent of the time spent in each area of your life in a typical week.

Areas of My Life	Activities I Engage in in a Typical Week	%
Ex: Sports	*Track, swimming, hiking, physical ed.*	*25%*
Sports		
Working		
Hanging out with friends		
Family Activities		
Time spent on a computer		
Time talking, e-mailing, texting, etc.		
Other		

(Continued on the next page)

SECTION I: JOURNALING ACTIVITIES

How I Spend My Time (continued)

When thinking about how you spend your time, it is important to look at the amount of time you spend in the various roles you play. Because you are called upon to play a variety of roles in life, making choices about how to spend your time is critical. Remember that some roles may be more important than others at any given point in time. Some of the roles you play are listed below. Describe how you spend time in each role. Then assign an estimated per cent of the time spent in each role per week.

My Roles	How I Spend This Time	%
Ex: Student	*Classes, chess club, homework, tutor*	*50%*
Student		
Employee		
Child		
Sibling		
Friend		
Volunteer		
Other		

SECTION I: JOURNALING ACTIVITIES

Making Effective Time Choices

Answer the following questions to help explore your time choices.

1. What activities do you most enjoy doing?

2. What fun activities would you like to do more often?

3. What type of career or occupation would you like to investigate? How can you do so?

4. What volunteer options might you like to consider?

(Continued on the next page)

SECTION I: JOURNALING ACTIVITIES

Making Effective Time Choices (continued)

5. What types of activities are you spending too much time on during the week?

___

6. What types of activities are you not spending enough time on during the week?

___

7. What surprised you most about your results on the assessment?

___

8. What did you learn about yourself from responding to the assessment?

___

SECTION I: JOURNALING ACTIVITIES

Each Week . . .

How do you spend your time being creative?
_____
_____
_____
_____

How do you spend your time being productive?
_____
_____
_____
_____

How do you spend your time being leisurely?
_____
_____
_____
_____

How do you spend your time being helpful to others?
_____
_____
_____
_____

How do you spend your time in self-reflection?
_____
_____
_____
_____

SECTION I: JOURNALING ACTIVITIES

You Can Do It!

What activity would you really like to try now?
_____
_____
_____
_____
_____
_____
_____
_____
_____
_____

What stands in your way?
_____
_____
_____
_____
_____
_____
_____
_____
_____

How can you make it happen?
_____
_____
_____
_____
_____
_____
_____
_____
_____

SECTION I: JOURNALING ACTIVITIES

Making Wise Choices
Quotations

These four quotes are related to various aspects of making effective time choices. Select one quote and write about how this it speaks to you based on something you have experienced in your life.

- ❑ *The world belongs to the energetic.* ~ **Ralph Waldo Emerson**

- ❑ *Ordinary people think of merely spending time. Great people think of using it.* ~ **Anonymous**

- ❑ *It's how we spend our time here and now, that really matters. If you are fed up with the way you have come to interact with it, change it.* ~ **Marcia Wieder**

- ❑ *Lost time is never found again.* ~ **Proverb**

_____
_____
_____
_____
_____
_____
_____
_____
_____
_____
_____
_____
_____
_____
_____
_____
_____

Section I: Journaling Activities

Teens & Time Management

Some of the ways teens can achieve more productivity out of their time:

- Keep a calendar current and with you at all times.

- In your calendar, have a "to-do" list and keep it current.

- In your "to-do" list, prioritize. Begin with what is most important.

- Lay-out or organize your clothes the night before school.

- At the end of the day, keep your keys, wallet, purse, back-pack in the same place – all together.

- Set your alarm 15 minutes early to avoid an early morning rush.

- Manage your time rather than trying to accommodate everything that comes your way.

- Remember, it is okay to say "no" to friends interested in activities that might distract you from what's important to you.

- Know that you cannot do everything. Focus on several activities you benefit from and enjoy.

- Be willing to say "no" when you feel like you simply don't have time.

SECTION II:
Teen Relationship Choices Scale

Name_____

Date_____

SECTION II: TEEN RELATIONSHIP CHOICES SCALE

Teen Relationship Choices Scale Directions

You have many different types of relationships in your life: acquaintances, friends, good friends or dating friends. It is important to explore your various relationships and why you make the relationship choices you make. The Relationship Choices Scale can help you identify and think about the characteristics you value in your relationship choices.

In the following example, the circled 3 indicates that the person in the example finds it somewhat easy to get emotionally close to others.

4 = Very Descriptive   **3 = Somewhat Descriptive**   **2 = A Little Descriptive**   **1 = Not At All Descriptive**

It is easy for me to get emotionally close to others 4   (3)   2   1

This is not a test, and there are no right or wrong answers. Do not spend too much time thinking about your answers. Your initial response will be the most true for you.
Be sure to respond to every statement.

(Turn to the next page and begin)

SECTION II: TEEN RELATIONSHIP CHOICES SCALE

Teen Relationship Choices Scale

4 = Very Descriptive **3 = Somewhat Descriptive** **2 = A Little Descriptive** **1 = Not At All Descriptive**

It is easy for me to get emotionally close to others	4	3	2	1
I am comfortable depending on others	4	3	2	1
I like having others depend on me	4	3	2	1
I don't worry about having others accept me	4	3	2	1
I can balance closeness and independence in a friendship	4	3	2	1
I feel my friends truly understand me	4	3	2	1
I find it easy to develop close relationships	4	3	2	1
I go to my friends in times of stress	4	3	2	1
I can share my thoughts and feelings with my friends	4	3	2	1
I enjoy sharing time with my friends	4	3	2	1

A TOTAL = _____

I want to be close to my friends	4	3	2	1
I often find that others don't get as close as I would like	4	3	2	1
I am uncomfortable without close friendships	4	3	2	1
I worry that my friends don't value me	4	3	2	1
I need approval from my friends	4	3	2	1
Some people say I am "clingy"	4	3	2	1
I often doubt my worth as a friend	4	3	2	1
I worry about my friends abandoning me	4	3	2	1
I worry that my friends do not like me as much as I like them	4	3	2	1
I prefer to have only a few very close relationships	4	3	2	1

B TOTAL = _____

(Continued on the next page)

SECTION II: TEEN RELATIONSHIP CHOICES SCALE

(Teen Relationship Choices Scale continued)

| 4 = Very Descriptive | 3 = Somewhat Descriptive | 2 = A Little Descriptive | 1 = Not At All Descriptive |

I am comfortable without close friends	4	3	2	1
It is important that I feel independent	4	3	2	1
I don't want to depend on others	4	3	2	1
I don't want others to depend on me	4	3	2	1
I don't need close relationships	4	3	2	1
I am uncomfortable getting close to others	4	3	2	1
I do not trust others completely	4	3	2	1
I hide my feelings around my friends	4	3	2	1
I feel uncomfortable when my friends reveal too much information about themselves	4	3	2	1
My friendships are often shallow	4	3	2	1

C TOTAL = _____

(Go to the Scoring Directions on the next page)

SECTION II: TEEN RELATIONSHIP CHOICES SCALE

Teen Relationship Choices Scale
Scoring Directions

The Relationship Choices Scale is designed to help you explore the ways in which you interact with acquaintances, friends and dating partners. Add your scores within each section of this scale. Record each total in the space provided after each section.

A. SECURE TOTAL _____

B. ANXIOUS TOTAL _____

C. INDEPENDENT TOTAL _____

Profile Interpretation

Total Scale Scores	Result	Indications
10 to 19	low	This is probably not your way of interacting with others.
20 to 30	moderate	This may be your way of interacting with others.
31 to 40	high	This is probably your way of interacting with others.

For scales which you scored in the **Moderate** or **High** range, find the descriptions on the pages that follow. Then, read the description and complete the exercises that are included. No matter how you scored, low, moderate or high, you will benefit from all of these exercises by learning more about your relationships.

Scale Descriptions are provided for the three scales you just completed.

SECTION II: TEEN RELATIONSHIP CHOICES SCALE

Secure

In this way of interacting, people believe that it is relatively easy for them to become emotionally close to others. They are comfortable in their friendships and enjoy depending on others and having others depend on them. They have a history of warm and caring relationships with people around them.

When referring to people you know, use a separate code for each, but not their initials.

(MLS = Marian Likes Sandwiches)

Describe how you are able to get emotionally close to other people.

_____
_____
_____
_____

With whom are you especially close? (use code names)

_____ _____ _____ _____
_____ _____ _____ _____

With whom have you developed equal give and take relationships?

_____ _____ _____ _____
_____ _____ _____ _____

With whom do you have relationships that are **not** equal give and take relationships. Check the person who is giving more than taking.

_____ _____ _____ _____
_____ _____ _____ _____

How has the secure way of interacting with your friends worked for or against you?

_____
_____
_____
_____

SECTION II: TEEN RELATIONSHIP CHOICES SCALE

Anxious

In this way of interacting, people often become preoccupied with wanting to have many friends and to develop close relationships with people. They are often concerned about their worth to their friends and worry that their friends are not being responsive enough to them. Use name codes.

Describe why you feel you need a lot of friends.

_____
_____
_____
_____
_____

With whom are you especially close? (use code names)

_____ _____ _____ _____
_____ _____ _____ _____

With whom have you developed equal give and take relationships?

_____ _____ _____ _____
_____ _____ _____ _____

With whom do you have relationships that are **not** equal give and take relationships. Check the person who is giving more than taking.

_____ _____ _____ _____
_____ _____ _____ _____

How has this anxious way of interacting with your friends worked for or against you?

_____
_____
_____
_____
_____

SECTION II: TEEN RELATIONSHIP CHOICES SCALE

Independent

In this style, people do not feel they need especially close friendships and relationships. They enjoy their independence and do not want to rely on other people. They view themselves as self-sufficient and may view close relationships as relatively unimportant. Use name codes.

Describe how you feel about your independence.

_____
_____
_____

What types of people do you usually befriend?

_____
_____

With whom are you especially close? (use code names)

_____ _____ _____ _____
_____ _____ _____ _____

With whom have you developed equal give and take relationships?

_____ _____ _____ _____
_____ _____ _____ _____

With whom do you have relationships that are **not** equal give and take relationships? Check the person who is giving more than taking.

_____ _____ _____ _____
_____ _____ _____ _____

How has the independent way of interacting with your friends worked for or against you?

_____
_____
_____

SECTION II: ACTIVITY HANDOUTS

Acquaintances

Who are your acquaintances and how would you describe them? In the following table, identify your acquaintances, describe how you interact with them, and explain why they are just acquaintances. Use name codes.

My Acquaintances	How I Interact with This Person	Why This Person Is Just an Acquaintance
❏ Ex: JBR	We smile and say "Hi" when we're in school, but that's it.	I have seen him bully some boys and I don't want him for a friend.
❏		
❏		
❏		
❏		
❏		
❏		

Which acquaintance would you like to get to know better? Put a check by their name codes. With which acquaintances are you satisfied to keep the relationship as is? Put an X by that acquaintance's name codes.

SECTION II: ACTIVITY HANDOUTS

Getting to Know You

We all have some acquaintances with whom we have no desire to become better friends. We also have some who would probably make great friends. What actions can you take to develop acquaintances into good friends? Use name codes.

I Want to Become Better Acquainted with . . .	How I Can Get to Know This Person
Ex: ZMW	I know he works out a lot. Maybe I can ask him if he'll show me his exercise routine.

SECTION II: ACTIVITY HANDOUTS

My Friends

Who are your friends (friends, not best friends) and how would you describe them? In the following table, identify your friends, describe who they are, and explain how you interact with them. Use name codes.

My Friends	How I Interact with This Person	Why This Person Is My Friend
Ex: BMC	We both like to party.	She and I have the same style of behaviour at a party.

Why do you remain friends?

_____

_____

_____

SECTION II: ACTIVITY HANDOUTS

Developing Positive Friendships

Friendships are relationships in which both people display support, warmth and caring for each other. List the ways you can begin to develop closer friendships with others.

Friendship Skills	How I Will Begin to Develop More Friendships
Honest & Trustworthy	
Supportive	
Tolerant	
Caring & Appreciative	
Respectful	

Ending Negative Friendships

Some relationships you are in have been developed based on negative behaviors and may not be serving you well. List the ways that you will end negative friendships with others.

Friendships Based On	How I Will End Negative Friendships
Negative Peer Pressure	
Bullying Behaviors	
Lying Behaviors	
Drugs and Alcohol Use	
Partying	

SECTION II: ACTIVITY HANDOUTS

Best Friends

Who are your best friends and how would you describe them? In the following table, identify your best friends, describe who they are and how you interact with them. Use name codes.

My Best Friends	How I Interact with This Person	Why This Person Is One of My Best Friends
Ex: ERA	We confide in and support each other.	I trust her completely. She brings out the best in me.

Why do these people continue to be your best friends?

_____

_____

_____

SECTION II: ACTIVITY HANDOUTS

Being A Better Friend

Everyone can benefit by developing more friends and being a better friend. In the following spaces, identify some of the actions you will take to create more good friend relationships.

Ways to Improve a Friendship	What I Will Do
Caring about each person	
Spending more time with each person	
Wanting what's best for each person	
Supporting each person in time of need	
Honesty	
Giving helpful feedback	
Other	

SECTION II: ACTIVITY HANDOUTS

Dating Friends

Who are the people you date, or have dated during the past six months, and how would you describe them? Below, identify them with a name code, describe who they are and how you interacted with them.

A Person I Date/Dated	How I Interact with This Person	Why I Like (or Liked) This Person
Ex: CHB	We go to the movies one night a week and get together to do homework a few times a week.	I am really busy with school and home. He is thoughtful and respects my choices.

What qualities do you look for in a person you are going to date?

_____ _____ _____
_____ _____ _____
_____ _____ _____

SECTION II: JOURNALING AVTIVITIES

Relationship Quotations

Choose two of the quotes below. Put a check by the one you like the most and an X by the one you liked the least. Write about why you selected them.

Shared joy is double joy; shared sorrow is half a sorrow.
   ~ Swedish Proverb

Remember, we all stumble, every one of us. That's why it's a comfort to go hand in hand.
   ~ Emily Kimbrough

Someone to tell it to is one of the fundamental needs of human beings.
   ~ Miles Franklin

In the coldest February, as in every month in every year, the best thing to hold on to in this world is each other.
   ~ Linda Ellerbee

✔ _____
_____
_____
_____
_____
_____
_____
_____

X _____
_____
_____
_____
_____
_____
_____
_____

SECTION II: JOURNALING ACTIVITIES

Journaling about Relationships

What have you enjoyed most about the acquaintances in your life?

_____

What do you most enjoy about being friends with other people?

_____

(Continued on the next page)

SECTION II: JOURNALING ACTIVITIES

Journaling about Relationships *(Continued)*

What do your best friends have in common?

_____
_____
_____
_____
_____
_____
_____
_____
_____
_____
_____
_____
_____
_____

What do you want most from a person you are dating?

_____
_____
_____
_____
_____
_____
_____
_____
_____
_____
_____
_____
_____

Developing New Relationships

- Start conversations based on mutual experiences and interests

- Take calculated risks in approaching others

- Discuss things you have in common

- Work on overcoming your shyness

- Maintain eye contact

- Show interest

- Listen

- Use open-ended questions

- Paraphrase or reflect thoughts and feelings to show you understand

Nurturing Long-Lasting Relationships

- Develop trust between each other

- Share emotions and thoughts as much as you feel comfortable

- Listen actively to the other person and truly hear and understand the messages being conveyed

- Allow friends to vent

- Support the person during difficult times

- Be honest

- Be reliable

- Be responsible

- Be non-judgmental

- Give suggestions and/or advice when asked

- Intervene if the person's safety is at risk

SECTION III:
Teen Cultural Differences Scale

Name_____

Date_____

SECTION III: TEEN CULTURAL DIFFERENCES SCALE

Teen Cultural Differences Scale Directions

Teens and adults see the world through the lens of their own cultural influences. By realizing that diversity in today's society is a reality and is desirable, we learn through others' wide experiences. People from different cultures come into contact and interact through travel, education and technology. Today, understanding and accepting people from different cultures becomes increasingly important. The Cultural Differences Scale is designed to help you make wise choices in assessing your openness and interest in befriending people who are different from you.

Read each of the statements that follow and decide how much the statement describes you. Then, circle the number of your response to the right of each statement.

In the following example, the circled number 2 indicates that the statement is Somewhat True for the person completing the assessment:

We define culture and diversity as differences in race, religion, spirituality, ethnicity, national origin, heritage, gender, color of skin, sexual orientation, older age, appearance, clothing, values, financial or social status, mental illness, and special physical and learning needs.

    3 = Very True   **2 = Somewhat True**   **1 = Not True**

1.
I respect the way people from different cultures view things
even though their views may be different from mine. 3 (2) 1

This is not a test and there are no right or wrong answers. Do not spend too much time thinking about your answers. Your initial response will be most true for you. Be sure to respond to every statement.

(Turn to the next page and begin)

SECTION III: TEEN CULTURAL DIFFERENCES SCALE

Teen Cultural Differences Scale

We define culture and diversity as differences in race, religion, spirituality, ethnicity, national origin, heritage, gender, color of skin, sexual orientation, older age, appearance, clothing, values, financial or social status, mental illness, and special physical and learning needs.

3 = Very True   2 = Somewhat True   1 = Not True

I.

I respect the way people from different cultures view things even though their views may be different from mine	3	2	1
I make an effort to get to know people from a variety of cultures	3	2	1
I have no prejudice toward people who are different from me	3	2	1
I am aware of how cultural differences and the way people grow up influence thoughts, behaviors, and communication	3	2	1
I accept other people's values	3	2	1
I do not stereotype people based on their culture	3	2	1

I - TOTAL = _____

II.

I am interested in knowing how my culture is viewed by others	3	2	1
I am interested in reading about other cultures	3	2	1
I am interested in learning about cultures different from my own	3	2	1
I enjoy talking with people who are different from me, and enjoy learning from them	3	2	1
I like to share my knowledge and experiences with people from other cultures	3	2	1
I would like to learn more about cultural norms, attitudes, and beliefs	3	2	1

II - TOTAL = _____

(Continued on the next page)

SECTION III: TEEN CULTURAL DIFFERENCES SCALE

(Teen Cultural differences Scale continued)

We define culture and diversity as differences in race, religion, spirituality, ethnicity, national origin, heritage, gender, color of skin, sexual orientation, older age, appearance, clothing, values, financial or social status, mental illness, and special physical and learning needs.

       3 = Very True   **2 = Somewhat True**   **1 = Not True**

III.

I like to introduce people of different cultures to my family and friends 3   2   1

I am aware of how my actions or words can affect people 3   2   1

I am able to make friends with anyone. 3   2   1

I am flexible and respect others' views, even if they are different
from my own 3   2   1

I can use a variety of verbal and nonverbal communication
in my interactions with people of cultures different from mine 3   2   1

I am flexible and respect other's views, even if they are different
from my own 3   2   1

III - TOTAL = _____

IV.

I like to establish friendships with people from different cultures 3   2   1

I would be willing to learn more about a friend's differences 3   2   1

I would attend a workshop to learn about the beliefs of a different culture 3   2   1

I feel very comfortable hanging out with people different from me 3   2   1

I enjoy working on projects with people who are from a different culture 3   2   1

I have and/or would like to attend cultural events, parades or festivals. 3   2   1

IV - TOTAL = _____

(Go to the Scoring Directions on the next page)

SECTION III: TEEN CULTURAL DIFFERENCES SCALE

Teen Cultural Differences Scale Scoring Directions

When choosing friends, teens often have to make choices based on how they respond to differences in others. To determine how you perceive differences in others, add the numbers you have circled for each of the four sections you just completed. You will get a number from 6 to 18. Put that total on the line marked total at the end of each section. Then, transfer your totals to the spaces below:

I = ATTITUDE _____

II = KNOWLEDGE _____

III = SKILLS _____

IV = VALUING DIVERSITY _____

Profile Interpretation

Total Scale Scores	Result	Indications
15 to 18	high	Scores from 15 to 18 on any single scale indicate that you currently possess many of the attitudes, knowledge, skills and values needed to recognize and appreciate diversity. Continue to develop the understanding, compassion and acceptance of people different from you.
10 to 14	moderate	Scores from 10 to 14 on any single scale indicate that you currently possess some of the attitudes, knowledge, skills and values needed to recognize and appreciate diversity. Continue to develop the understanding, compassion and acceptance of people different from you.
6 to 9	low	Scores from 6 to 9 on any single scale indicate that you do not currently possess the attitudes, knowledge, skills and values needed to recognize and appreciate diversity. You need to work on developing effective understanding, compassion and acceptance of people different from you.

SECTION III: TEEN CULTURAL DIFFERENCES SCALE

Teen Cultural Differences Scale Profile Descriptions

Following are descriptions of the four scales included on the assessment. Remember that as globalization becomes the norm, it is important for you to develop an appreciation and an understanding of people from different walks of life.

Attitudes

People scoring low on this scale have not experienced or learned the importance of curiosity, empathy and respect in cross-cultural communications. They may still have some stereotypes of particular cultures based on past influences and experiences, and they do not make much of an effort to learn about other cultures.

Knowledge

People scoring low on this scale have not experienced or developed an interest in learning about the customs and traditions of other cultures. They do not have an interest in choosing to share with or learn about people from other cultures.

Skills

People scoring low on this scale may not have the desire to make friends with people from other cultures. They may be rigid about their beliefs of people from other cultures, and may have difficulty valuing others' views and opinions or communicating with them.

Valuing Diversity

People scoring low on this scale have difficulty accepting and respecting differences in people. They have a hard time accepting that people come from very different backgrounds, and that their values, traditions, ways of communicating, thoughts and abilities as well as customs differ.

The following sections contain exercises to help you choose to build relationships with people different from you. Regardless of your scores on the assessment, these exercises will help you to make better choices about friends and being a better citizen in global interactions.

SECTION III: ACTIVITY HANDOUTS

Valuing Diversity

Recognizing that diversity exists and being able to value the fundamental differences that exist in people is a requirement for living successfully in today's world. You may have some friends who are different from you or you may lack friends from diverse cultures. One way to accomplish this is to recognize that cultural diversity exists and learn to value and respect the many types of differences that people possess. In the table below, list some of the fundamental benefits of having diverse friends in the left-hand column and list the drawbacks of having diverse friends in the right-hand column. Use name codes.

Benefits of Diverse Friends	Drawbacks of Diverse Friends
Ex: TJ and I have computers in common; something he is really good at because of his learning disability. I learn from him each time we're together!	Ex: We sometimes spend too much time alone at the library on computers, alienating ourselves from others in class.

Interact With Diverse Individuals

To increase your cultural understanding, you need to begin or continue to interact with people who are different from you. When people who have a mutual interest are brought together, they automatically begin to form a relationship that will dissolve stereotypes and enhance cooperative interaction. In the table below, list some of the people (from work, school, place of worship, community, etc.) whom you would like to get to know better. In the column on the left, list these people and in the column to the right, list an activity, project, or mutual goal that you and the other person could work toward. Then, try out your plan.

Person I Would Like to Get to Know	Project, Activity, Common Interest We Could Possibly Work On
Ex: MRC is in a wheelchair and seems to be such a nice person. He doesn't seem to have many friends.	Ex: I can ask the teacher to buddy me up with him for a 2-person project in science class.

SECTION III: ACTIVITY HANDOUTS

Your Own Cultural Identity

To appreciate the unique heritage of others, you may need to develop an appreciation of your own cultural and ethnic identity. To better appreciate the cultural aspects of others and build effective relationships with people different from you, you need to appreciate your own culture. In the spaces below, identify some of the characteristics that make you unique.

Personal Identity	How It Makes Me Unique
Country where I was born	
My religious / spiritual upbringing	
My gender	
My age	
My health	
My family's socio-economic status	
My family's traditions	

SECTION III: ACTIVITY HANDOUTS

Avoid Stereotyping

A stereotype is a fixed impression of someone, or a set of exaggerated or preconceived ideas about a particular group of people. Some outcomes of stereotypical behavior serve as a foundation for discrimination, hatred, judgmental comments, prejudice and bullying of people who are different from you. They may have a different race, religion, spirituality, ethnicity, national origin, heritage, gender, skin color, sexual orientation or older age. Their appearance, clothing, values, financial or social status may be different from yours. They may have a mental illness, physical or learning disabilities.

Stereotypes usually surface in these ways:

- Simplified negative or positive ideas about a person
- Overgeneralizations that do not represent all members of a group
- Attempts to enhance one's own self-esteem

To practice minimizing and changing possible stereotyping, think about people in your life who might be different from you and about whom you might have had preconceived thoughts. (Refer to the list in the first paragraph.) How can you get to know them better? They might be from school, your neighborhood, community, place of worship, volunteer or work place, etc. Use name codes.

People Who Are Different From Me	How I Can Get to Know Them Better

SECTION III: ACTIVITY HANDOUTS

My Stereotypes

Now is the time to clarify the different kinds of stereotypes you may believe. Think about the stereotypes that you believe and some of the people with whom you typically interact. In the left column are some groups that have stereotypes associated with them. In the right column, identify and list some of your stereotypical thinking, associated with those groups.

Groups (Use group codes)	My Stereotypes – Positive or Negative
Males	
Females	
My Race/Color	
Other Races/Colors	
My Religion	
Other religions	
My Ethnicity	
Other Ethnicities	

(Continued on the next page)

SECTION III: ACTIVITY HANDOUTS

My Stereotypes (continued)

Groups (Use group codes)	My Stereotypes – Positive or Negative
Special Needs Students	
Gender Identities	
People with a different sexual orientation	
Senior Citizens	
People of a different Socio-economic status from mine	
People born in other countries who speak a different language than I do	
People who have low-paying jobs or no jobs.	
Other	
Other	
Other	

SECTION III: ACTIVITY HANDOUTS

People from Other Countries

It is an important decision to learn to make friends with people from different geographical areas. To have varied, interesting friendships, it helps to become more aware of cultural differences among people and places. Think about how you might learn more about other cultures. In the table that follows, list some of the strategies you might use to learn more about other cultures of the world.

Ways to Learn about Other Countries	Strategies
Ex: Visit other countries.	Ex: Find a school trip that will be touring another country. Take some jobs to raise money to go on the trip. If needed, ask for financial assistance.
Visit other countries.	
Attend a place of worship with someone from a different country.	
Learn enough words of a foreign language to be able to communicate.	
Read about other countries and their traditions.	
Talk to people from another culture and ask questions. Share about your culture.	
Attend cultural festivals.	

SECTION III: ACTIVITY HANDOUTS

People with a Different Sexual Orientation

To overcome stereotyping, you can choose to become acquainted with people who have a different sexual orientation from yours. To have varied, interesting relationships and friendships, it helps to become more aware of your perceptions related to people with a different sexual orientation. In the table that follows, list some of the perceptions that you have about people with a different sexual orientation, and then describe ways you can overcome any negative perceptions. Use name or group code.

Person (name code) or **Group of People** (group code)	My Perceptions/Feelings	How I Will Attempt to Overcome My Perceptions/Feelings

SECTION III: ACTIVITY HANDOUTS

People with Special Needs or Health Issues

To overcome stereotyping, you can choose to become acquainted with people who have special needs. To have varied, interesting relationships and friendships, it helps to become more aware of your perceptions of special needs people. In the table that follows, list some of the perceptions that you have about special needs people, and then describe ways you can overcome any negative perceptions. Use name code or group code.

Person (name code) **or Group of People** (group code)	**My Perceptions/Feelings**	**How I Will Attempt to Overcome My Perceptions/Feelings**

SECTION III: ACTIVITY HANDOUTS

People from a Different Race or Religion

To overcome stereotyping, you can choose to become acquainted with people who are of a different race and/or religion. To have varied, interesting relationships and friendships, it helps to become more aware of your perceptions related to people with different skin color or religious beliefs. In the table that follows, list some of the perceptions that you have about them, and then describe ways you can overcome any negative perceptions.

Person (name code) or **Group of People** (group code)	My Perceptions/Feelings	How I Will Attempt to Overcome My Perceptions/Feelings

SECTION III: ACTIVITY HANDOUTS

People in a Different Financial Situation

To overcome stereotyping, you can choose to become acquainted with people of a financial situation different from yours. To have varied, interesting relationships and friendships, it helps to become more aware of your perceptions related to people who come from families of a different social class. In the table that follows, list some of the perceptions that you have about people from different social classes, and then describe ways you can overcome any negative perceptions. Use name code.

Person (name code) or Group of People (group code)	**My Perceptions/Feelings**	**How I Will Attempt to Overcome My Perceptions/Feelings**

SECTION III: JOURNALING ACTIVITIES

What I Learned About Myself

What have you learned about yourself and how you interact with people different from you?
_____
_____
_____
_____
_____
_____
_____
_____
_____
_____

What have you learned about people from other cultures and how they interact with you?
_____
_____
_____
_____
_____
_____
_____
_____
_____
_____

What choices can you make to create a culturally friendly and non-prejudicial life?
_____
_____
_____
_____
_____
_____
_____
_____
_____
_____

The Cycle of Hatred

Stereotypes
Positive or negative beliefs held by an individual about a group of people.

Prejudices
A judgment, feeling, or attitude based on a belief about a cultural or other type of group.

Discrimination
A negative behavior toward a person or persons based on this judgment, feeling, or attitude.

SECTION III: JOURNALING ACTIVITIES

The Cycle of Hatred Quotations

Write your thoughts on each of these quotations regarding the three elements of
The Cycle of Hatred

Stereotypes – Prejudices – Discrimination

Stereotypes are devices for saving a biased person the trouble of learning.
   ~Unknown Source

_____
_____
_____
_____
_____

I have no race prejudice. I think I have no color prejudices or caste prejudices nor creed prejudices. Indeed, I know it. I can stand any society. All that I care to know is that a man is a human being – that is enough for me; he can't be any worse.
   ~ Mark Twain

_____
_____
_____
_____
_____

And each of us can practice rights ourselves, treating each other without discrimination, respecting each other's dignity and rights.
   ~ Carol Bellamy

_____
_____
_____
_____
_____

SECTION IV:
Teen "Not-So-Great" Choices Scale

Name_____

Date_____

SECTION IV: TEEN "NOT-SO-GREAT" CHOICES SCALE

Teen "Not-So-Great" Choices Scale Directions

Decision making is an important life skill. Teens can make bad choices for a variety of reasons, including not thinking the choice through, acting impulsively, caving in to peer pressure, and pushing to achieve greater independence.

The *My "not-so-great" Choices Scale* can help you explore the factors that influenced bad choices you have made in the past. This scale contains 32 statements. Read each of the statements and decide how much you agree with the statement. In each of the choices listed, circle the number of your response on the line to the right of each statement.

In the following example, the circled 4 indicates that the statement is **Very True** of the person completing the scale:

	Very True	True	Somewhat True	Not True
1. I did not think it through	(4)	3	2	1

This is not a test and there are no right or wrong answers. Do not spend too much time thinking about your answers. Your initial response will be the most true for you. Be sure to respond to every statement.

Think about a choice you have made in the past that did not work out well for you. Complete the assessment based on this situation.

My "not-so-great" choice was _____
_____
_____
_____

(Turn to the next page and begin)

SECTION IV: TEEN "NOT-SO-GREAT" CHOICES SCALE

Teen "Not-So-Great" Choices Scale

	Very True	True	Somewhat True	Not True
1. I did not think it through	4	3	2	1
2. I acted on the spur of the moment	4	3	2	1
3. I wanted to fit in with my friends	4	3	2	1
4. I wanted to defy my parents	4	3	2	1
5. I did not consider the consequences of my actions	4	3	2	1
6. I made up my mind too quickly	4	3	2	1
7. Everyone was doing it	4	3	2	1
8. I wanted to be more in control in my life	4	3	2	1
9. I did not think long-term	4	3	2	1
10. I felt like I needed to do something	4	3	2	1
11. I was encouraged by others	4	3	2	1
12. I wanted to test my boundaries	4	3	2	1
13. I did not think about the available choices	4	3	2	1
14. I rushed	4	3	2	1
15. I felt pressured by others	4	3	2	1
16. I wanted to defy my parents and their authority	4	3	2	1
17. I couldn't interpret all of the information available	4	3	2	1
18. It sounded good at the time	4	3	2	1
19. I wanted to show others I could	4	3	2	1
20. I wanted to challenge my parents values	4	3	2	1
21. I did not have a logical decision-making plan in place	4	3	2	1
22. It did not seem risky	4	3	2	1
23. I wanted to be accepted	4	3	2	1
24. I wanted to see how my parents would react	4	3	2	1
25. I could not think logically	4	3	2	1
26. I simply reacted	4	3	2	1
27. I didn't want to seem like a baby	4	3	2	1
28. I wanted to rebel	4	3	2	1
29. I saw limited options available to me	4	3	2	1
30. I had a strong feeling I should do it	4	3	2	1
31. I didn't want my peers to think badly of me	4	3	2	1
32. I wanted to feel more grown up	4	3	2	1

(Go to the Scoring Directions on the next page)

SECTION IV: TEEN "NOT-SO-GREAT" CHOICES SCALE

Teen "Not-So-Great" Choices Scale Scoring

You have, and will continue, to face many important decisions in your life. The purpose of this assessment is to help you explore the factors that have influenced bad decisions you have made in the past. The *My "Not-So-Great" Choices Scale* is designed to measure several aspects that may have influenced you in the decision-making process:

- **Critical Thinking**
- **Impulsive Behavior**
- **Peer Pressure**
- **Independence Status**

The scoring process groups items into the above four scales to allow you to explore your decision-making style.

Use the spaces below to record the number which you circled on each individual item of the assessment.

Score	Score	Score	Score
1_____	2_____	3_____	4_____
5_____	6_____	7_____	8_____
9_____	10_____	11_____	12_____
13_____	14_____	15_____	16_____
17_____	18_____	19_____	20_____
21_____	22_____	23_____	24_____
25_____	26_____	27_____	28_____
29_____	30_____	31_____	32_____
Critical Thinking	**Impulsive Behavior**	**Peer Pressure**	**Independent Status**
Total = _____	Total = _____	Total = _____	Total = _____

(Go to the Profile Interpretation on the next page)

SECTION IV: TEEN "NOT-SO-GREAT" CHOICES SCALE

Teen "Not-So-Great" Choices Scale Profile Interpretation

Total Individual Scales Scores	Result	Indications
8 to 15	low	You tend to make most of your choices based on factors in a logical, well-thought-out system for decision making.
16 to 24	moderate	You tend to make some of your choices based on factors in a logical, well-thought-out system for decision making.
25 to 32	high	You tend to make few or none of your choices based on factors in a logical, well-thought-out system for decision making.

On the next page is information about the specific scales on which you scored. Whether you scored low, moderate or high, you will benefit from doing the exercises on the following pages.

SECTION IV: TEEN "NOT-SO-GREAT" CHOICES SCALE

Teen "Not-So-Great" Choices Scale
Scale Descriptions

Critical Thinking Scale

Teens scoring high on this scale tend to lack the necessary critical thinking skills to make logical decisions, think through the situation, understand their anticipated choice, and think about possible outcomes and consequences.

Impulsive Behavior Scale

Teens scoring high on this scale tend to act impulsively and make decisions based on their emotions in an illogical and not very well-thought out plan. They want instant gratification and do not think through their actions.

Peer Pressure Scale

Teens scoring high on this scale tend to give in to social pressures of their peers. They tend to be susceptible to other teens who encourage them to make certain decisions or behave in certain ways. They want to fit in with their peers, so they tend to go along with behaviors they may not do normally.

Independent Status Scale

Teens scoring high on this scale tend to make decisions in an effort to assert their independence from their parents' and other adults' values, rules and authority. They feel the need to test their boundaries and struggle for autonomy. They feel they are grown up and want to think and act independently.

The following exercises have been designed to help you develop a logical decision-making system for making choices. Engage in all of the exercises and activities that follow and practice the ones which you feel will help you make effective choices, no matter how you scored, low, moderate or high.

SECTION IV: ACTIVITY HANDOUTS

Past "Not-So-Good" Choices

In the following table, list some of choices you made in the past that didn't work out very well, and then describe how these choices have affected your life so far. Use name codes.

Not-So-Good Choices I Have Made	How It Affected My Life
Ex: BG asked me to go out on a school night when I was supposed to do homework. I snuck out of the house.	I got caught and was grounded for a month! My parents still don't trust me completely.

How do you feel you have grown from these choices?

_____

_____

_____

SECTION IV: ACTIVITY HANDOUTS

Critical Thinking

Think about some of the situations in which you did not consider the consequences of your actions and did not think through your decisions. Describe those situations below.

Choices Made When I Did Not Think Things Through	The Result of That Not-So-Good Choice
Ex: A friend offered me a cigarette. I took it and continued to smoke with him. I wanted to be friends.	I became addicted to smoking. I hadn't thought about how my breath would smell and potential long-term health issues.

SECTION IV: ACTIVITY HANDOUTS

A Logical Decision-Making Process

The following is a logical decision-making process you can use when making important choices in your life:

1. Identify the decision to be made.
   (Ex: whether to drink alcohol at the party)

2. Identify the potential choices to be made.
   (Ex: go to the party and not drink, go to the party and drink, don't go to the party at all, etc.)

3. Identify and compare all of the possible consequences of the choices.
   (Ex: go to the party and have fun without drinking, go to the party and drink and possibly get into trouble, stay home and do something else)

4. Make a responsible decision based on all of the information you have available.
   (Ex: go to the party and have fun without drinking)

5. Act on your decision and evaluate the results.
   (Ex: went to the party and did not drink. Had a good time dancing and enjoyed myself without alcohol)

Your turn – Now you try it!

1. Identify an important choice you have coming up in the near future. What is that situation?

   _____
   _____
   _____
   _____
   _____

2. Identify the potential choices to be made.

   _____
   _____
   _____
   _____
   _____

(Continued on the next page)

SECTION IV: ACTIVITY HANDOUTS

A Logical Decision-Making Process *(Continued)*

3. Identify and compare all of the possible consequences of the choices.

_____
_____
_____
_____
_____
_____

4. Make a responsible decision based on all of the information you have available.

_____
_____
_____
_____
_____
_____

5. Now, how will you act on your decision.

_____
_____
_____
_____
_____
_____

What do you anticipate the results to be?

_____
_____
_____
_____
_____

SECTION IV: ACTIVITY HANDOUTS

Impulsive Behavior

Think about some of the situations in which you made decisions impulsively or based on emotion rather than a logical process. Describe those situations below.

An Impulsive Choice I Made	The Result of That No-So-Good Choice
Ex: I tried an illegal substance at a party.	Got busted!

Peer Pressure

Think about some of the situations in which you felt pressured to do something you did not want to do. Describe those situations below.

Choices I Made When Pressured By My Peers	The Result of That No-So-Good Choice
Ex: I raced with my car.	I had a car accident. I hurt the car, myself, and someone else, too!

SECTION IV: ACTIVITY HANDOUTS

Peer Pressure in Your Life

Why do you believe you give in to peer pressure?

_____
_____
_____
_____
_____

What are some things you can do to avoid being pressured by your peers? (be comfortable saying no, choose new friends, etc.)

_____
_____
_____
_____
_____

What would happen if you did not give in to that peer pressure?

_____
_____
_____
_____

How can you respond the next time your peers want you to do something you do not want to do?

1. _____
_____

2. _____
_____

3. _____
_____

SECTION IV: ACTIVITY HANDOUTS

Independent Status

Think about some of the situations in which you made choices based on your need to become more independent. Describe those situations below.

Choices I Made to Be More Independent	The Result of That No-So-Good Choice
Ex: I refuse to go on a family vacation. I stayed with a friend.	Her parents were stricter than mine. My whole family had a fabulous time – without me!

SECTION IV: ACTIVITY HANDOUTS

Your Independent Status

List one situation where you chose to be independent and the choice was not-so-great.

What were you trying to prove to your parents/caregivers?
_____
_____
_____

How did it feel to rebel?
_____
_____
_____

What were the consequences of this behavior?
_____
_____
_____
_____

What are some more positive ways to express your independence?
_____
_____
_____
_____

How did your parents/caregivers react to this choice?
_____
_____
_____
_____

SECTION IV: ACTIVITY HANDOUTS

Critical Thinking

Journal about how you can go through a logical process to make effective choices.

_____
_____
_____
_____
_____
_____
_____
_____
_____
_____
_____
_____
_____
_____
_____
_____
_____

Journal about how you can to curb your impulsivity when making important choices.

_____
_____
_____
_____
_____
_____
_____
_____
_____
_____
_____
_____
_____
_____
_____
_____

SECTION IV: JOURNALING ACTIVITIES

Peer Pressure

Journal about how you can react when you are pressured to do things you don't want to.
_____
_____
_____
_____
_____
_____
_____
_____
_____
_____
_____
_____
_____

Journal about how you can prove your independence.
_____
_____
_____
_____
_____
_____
_____
_____
_____
_____
_____
_____

Choice Quotations

To decide, to be at the level of choice, is to take responsibility for your life and to be in control of your life.
   ~ Abbie M. Dale

The strongest principle of growth lies in human choice.
   ~ George Eliot

It's about making wise choices among the things we now have to choose from.
   ~ Elaine St. James

It's choice – not chance – that determines your destiny.
   ~ Jean Nidetch

In every single thing you do, you are choosing a direction. Your life is a product of choices.
   ~ Kathleen Hall

Journal your thoughts about any of the above quotations and why it appeals to you.

_____
_____
_____
_____
_____
_____
_____
_____
_____
_____
_____
_____
_____
_____
_____

Important Decisions

Important decisions teens have to make include:

- Should I stay in school or drop out?
- What kind of a job am I qualified to do?
- What do I want to do after graduation?
- Who do I want to have as friends?
- Who do I want to date?
- When and with whom do I want to be intimate?
- Should I drink alcohol?
- Should I smoke cigarettes? Cigars? Chew tobacco?
- Should I try drugs or unhealthy substances?
- Should I steal? Shoplift?
- Should I join a gang?
- What occupation do I hope to pursue?
- Should I help someone who is being bullied?
- Should I confide in an adult that I am, or someone else is being bullied?
- Is it okay to break friends' confidences if they tell me they are thinking of hurting themselves?

Questions to Ask When Facing a Decision

- What am I really deciding?
- How will this affect me in the future?
- How will others be affected by my decision?
- Is the decision reversible?
- What are the long-term consequences of the decision?
- How can I avoid being impulsive in making the decision?
- What realistic outcome best serves me?
- What have I learned in the past that can help me make a decision?
- Is the outcome compatible with my values?
- What is the negative risk involved in the decision?

SECTION V:
Teen Risk-Taking Behavior Scale

Name_____

Date_____

SECTION V: TEEN RISK-TAKING BEHAVIOR SCALE

Teen Risk-Taking Behavior Scale Directions

Risk-taking, by its very nature, carries with it the potential for both loss and gain. Some risks can be beneficial to you, and others can cause undue stress, strain and danger in your life. The Risk-Taking Scale can help you to identify the ways in which you have taken risks in the past, and prepare you for risks that will occur in your future.

This section includes two scales
- **Positive Risk-Taking Behavior**
- **Negative Risk-Taking Behavior**

Each scale contains 20 statements. On both scales, read each of the statements and circle the number next to the statement that describes you.

In the following examples, the circled 2 indicates that both statements occur SOMETIMES for the person completing the scale.

Example – Positive Risk-Taking Scale

	Often	Sometimes	Never
In the past . . .			
I took a class I knew would be difficult for me	3	(2)	1

Example – Negative Risk-Taking Scale

	Often	Sometimes	Never
In the past . . .			
I experimented with illegal drugs	3	(2)	1

This is not a test and there are no right or wrong answers. Do not spend too much time thinking about your answers. Your initial response will likely be the most true for you. Be sure to respond to every statement.

(Turn to the next page and begin)

SECTION V: TEEN RISK-TAKING BEHAVIOR SCALE

Teen Positive Risk-Taking Behavior Scale

	Often	Sometimes	Never
In the past			
I took a class I knew would be difficult for me	3	2	1
I found ways to be involved in school activities	3	2	1
I opted for a class I knew nothing about	3	2	1
I joined a new club or organization at school	3	2	1
I tutored someone else	3	2	1

I - TOTAL = _____

	Often	Sometimes	Never
In the past . . .			
I volunteered to help other people	3	2	1
I applied for a part-time job	3	2	1
I helped others achieve their goals	3	2	1
I joined in various social activities	3	2	1
I started to date	3	2	1

II - TOTAL = _____

	Often	Sometimes	Never
In the past . . .			
I tried new hobbies	3	2	1
I attempted to learn about new cultures	3	2	1
I joined an exercise, fitness or wellness program	3	2	1
I learned or tried new sports	3	2	1
I tried a creative or artistic project	3	2	1

III - TOTAL = _____

	Often	Sometimes	Never
In the past . . .			
I assisted someone with homework	3	2	1
I did something unexpected and kind for a relative	3	2	1
I tried to communicate better with family members	3	2	1
I made friends with someone different from me	3	2	1
I helped someone being bullied	3	2	1

IV - TOTAL = _____

(Go to the Scoring Directions on the next page)

SECTION V: TEEN RISK-TAKING BEHAVIOR SCALE

Teen Positive Risk-Taking Behavior Scale Scoring Directions

Positive risk-taking can take many forms. For each of the four sections on the previous page, total the number of answers you circled for each section. Put that total on the line marked TOTAL at the end of each section.

Transfer your totals to the spaces below:

I	=	School	TOTAL =	_____
II	=	Social	TOTAL =	_____
III	=	Activities	TOTAL =	_____
IV	=	Family / Friends	TOTAL =	_____

Add your overall total = _____

Profile Interpretation

Individual Scales Scores	Total Score All Six Scales	Result	Indications
12 to 15	49 to 60	high	If you score high on any individual scale or all scales, you are **definitely** taking positive risks in your life.
9 to 11	34 to 48	moderate	If you score moderate on any individual scale or all scales, you are taking **some** positive risks in your life
5 to 8	20 to 33	low	If you score low on any or all scales, you are **not** taking very many positive risks in your life.

No matter how you scored, low, moderate or high, you will benefit from the following exercises.

SECTION V: ACTIVITY HANDOUTS

Positive Risks at School

What were some of the positive risks you took related to school and education? In the left-hand column, list the positive risk you took. Then describe the outcome of your risk and what you learned. Use name codes.

Positive Risks I Took	What Was the Outcome	What I Learned
Ex: I made an appointment and went to the school counselor, ML, to discuss grants and loans for college.	She was able to help me research.	Even though I was concerned about the outcome, I needed to take the first step.

How has your life improved through taking these positive risks?

_____
_____
_____

Positive Risks in My Social Life

What were some of the positive risks you took related to your social life?

In the left-hand column, list the positive risk you took.

Then describe the outcome of your risk and what you learned. Use name codes.

Positive Risks I Took	What Was the Outcome	What I Learned
Ex: I asked SAB for a date, even though I knew she'd say no.	She said yes!	It doesn't hurt to try. It was worth the risk.

How has your life improved through taking these positive risks?

_____

_____

_____

SECTION V: ACTIVITY HANDOUTS

Positive Risks in My Activities

What were some of the positive risks you took related to new activities in your life?
In the left-hand column, list the positive risk you took.
Then describe the outcome of your risk and what you learned. Use name codes.

Positive Risks I Took	What Was the Outcome	What I Learned

How has your life improved through taking these positive risks?
___
___
___

Positive Risks with My Family and Friends

What were some of the positive risks you took related to family and friends?

In the left-hand column, list the positive risks you took.

Then describe the outcome of your risks and what you learned. Use name codes.

Positive Risks I Took	What Was the Outcome	What I Learned
Ex: I was angry at MD and I asked if we could talk. I told him why I was angry.	He listened and understood what I said and then gave me his point of view. We compromised.	It was better to talk with him than hold it in and not be nice to him.

How has your life improved through taking these positive risks?

_____

_____

_____

SECTION V: ACTIVITY HANDOUTS

Positive Risks in the Future

Now think about some of the positive risks you have yet to take, and would like to take in the future. In the first column, list the positive risks you would like to take. Then, list what you need to do to take the positive risks and what you expect the outcome of the risks to be. Use name codes.

Positive Risks I Want to Take	What I Need to Do	What is the Expected Outcome
Ex: I want to travel to see my cousin. It will cost more money than I have.	Talk to my family and ask for suggestions on how I can earn money.	I think they will have some ideas and I will be able to go.

SECTION V: TEEN RISK-TAKING BEHAVIOR SCALE

Teen Negative Risk-Taking Behavior Scale

	Often	Sometimes	Never
In the past . . .			
I experimented with illegal drugs	3	2	1
I encouraged a friend to drink alcohol	3	2	1
I drove after drinking alcohol	3	2	1
I used tobacco products	3	2	1
I engaged in binge drinking	3	2	1

V - TOTAL = _____

	Often	Sometimes	Never
In the past . . .			
I bullied others	3	2	1
I became friendly with gang members or joined a gang	3	2	1
I took unnecessary physical risks	3	2	1
I hurt / mutilated myself	3	2	1
I have been in fights	3	2	1

VI - TOTAL = _____

	Often	Sometimes	Never
In the past . . .			
I carried a weapon	3	2	1
I got into trouble with the law	3	2	1
I vandalized	3	2	1
I hurt animals or people	3	2	1
I promoted hatred against other people	3	2	1

VII - TOTAL = _____

	Often	Sometimes	Never
In the past . . .			
I took steroids to build muscles	3	2	1
I engaged in unprotected sex	3	2	1
I had suicidal thoughts	3	2	1
I got a tattoo under unsanitary conditions	3	2	1
I gained / lost weight in an unhealthy way	3	2	1

VIII - TOTAL = _____

(Go to the Scoring Directions on the next page)

SECTION V: TEEN RISK-TAKING BEHAVIOR SCALE

Teen Negative Risk-Taking Behavior Scale Scoring Directions

People take negative risks for a variety of reasons. For each of the four sections on the previous page, total the number of answers you circled for each section. Put that total on the line marked TOTAL at the end of each section.

Transfer your totals to the spaces below:

      V = Substances TOTAL = _____

      VI = Physical TOTAL = _____

      VII = Criminal TOTAL = _____

      VIII = Health TOTAL = _____

      Add your overall total = _____

Profile Interpretation

Individual Scales Scores	Total Score All Six Scales	Result	Indications
12 to 15	49 to 60	high	If you score high on any individual scale or all scales, you are **definitely** taking negative risks in your life.
9 to 11	34 to 48	moderate	If you score moderate on any individual scale or all scales, you are taking **some** negative risks in your life
5 to 8	20 to 33	low	If you score low on any or all scales, you are **not** taking very many negative risks in your life.

No matter how you scored, low, moderate or high, you will benefit from the following exercises.

Negative Risks with Substances

What were some of the negative risks you took related to substances?

In the left-hand column, list the negative risks you took.

Then describe the outcome of your risks and what you learned. Use name codes.

Negative Risks I Took	The Outcome Was	What I Learned
Ex: I started using an unhealthy/illegal substance.	I became dependent on it, stole money, and got in a lot of trouble with my parents and the police.	I should never have started!

How has your life been hurt through taking these negative risks?

_____

_____

_____

SECTION V: ACTIVITY HANDOUTS

Negative Physical Risks

What were some of the negative risks you took related to physical activities?

In the left-hand column, list the negative risks you took.

Then describe the outcome of your risks and what you learned. Use name codes.

Negative Risks I Took	The Outcome Was	What I Learned
Ex: I watched JRS who was bullied by BB and I did nothing. I just stood there.	BB thought I was interested in being his friend, and I didn't. Then he bullied me, too.	I won't be a bystander anymore. I'll leave and tell someone.

How has your life been hurt through taking these negative risks?

_____

_____

SECTION V: ACTIVITY HANDOUTS

Negative Criminal Risks

What were some of the negative risks you took related to criminal activities?

In the left-hand column, list the negative risks you took.

Then describe the outcome of your risks and what you learned. Use name codes.

Negative Risks I Took	The Outcome Was	What I Learned
Ex: I brought a weapon to school to impress some people.	Someone in the hall saw it, was frightened, and reported me.	Carrying a weapon is dangerous and frightens people. I was in trouble with the police, school, some good friends, and my family.

How has your life been hurt through taking these negative risks?

_____

_____

_____

SECTION V: ACTIVITY HANDOUTS

Negative Health Risks

What were some of the negative risks you took related to your health?

In the left-hand column, list the negative risks you took.

Then describe the outcome of your risks and what you learned. Use name codes.

Negative Risks I Took	The Outcome Was	What I Learned
Ex: I starved myself for three days to lose weight.	On the fourth day, I had a stomach ache, ate everything in sight, and wound up gaining 5 pounds.	I'll find out about healthy eating plans from my health teacher or physical education instructor.

How has your life been hurt through taking these negative risks?

_____

_____

_____

SECTION V: ACTIVITY HANDOUTS

Learning about Negative Risks

All teens take risks as a normal part of growing up and exploring the world. Healthy risk-taking can help you grow, develop, and discover your identity. However, negative risk-taking behaviors can be harmful and even dangerous. Think about some of the times you have engaged in negative risk-taking behavior. Then try to describe what the motivation behind taking the risk was. Use name codes.

List a specific time you took negative risks _____

What Prompted the Negative Risk	How This Led (or Could Have Led) to Problems	I Learned . . .
Ex: Bad feelings about yourself.	*In front of other kids I ridiculed a gay person. She became very depressed and tried to hurt herself.*	*Not to judge others and hurt their feelings.*
Bad feelings about yourself		
Little or no self-confidence		
Peer Pressure		
Loneliness		
Wanting and/or needing to be liked and accepted		
Rebellion		
Striving for Independence		
Fear of your friends' reactions		
Thrill seeking		

SECTION V: JOURNALING ACTIVITIES

Motivations

What are your motivations to take positive risks?

What are your motivations to take negative risks?

Risk-Taking Quotations

Only those who dare to fail greatly can ever achieve greatly.
    ~ Robert F. Kennedy

The risks you take should be positive. They should not put you, or others, at risk of physical or emotional harm.
    ~ Gary Leboff

Journal your thoughts about either of the above quotations and how it applies to you.

_____
_____
_____
_____
_____
_____
_____
_____
_____
_____
_____
_____
_____
_____
_____
_____
_____
_____
_____
_____

Positive Risk-Taking

Teens can take positive risks in many different ways:

- Accept people different from you
- Act with respect to family and all adults
- Be assertive (not passive, not aggressive)
- Become responsible
- Belong to school, community or house of worship groups or clubs
- Do volunteer work
- Eat and drink healthy food and beverages
- Exercise
- Find a part-time job
- Follow rules
- Help others
- Join a school service group
- Meet new people
- Participate in sports
- Use your voice to report bullies, to help the person being bullied and to help someone in trouble (including yourself)

Negative Risk-Taking

Teens can take negative risks in many different ways:

- Act in ways you know you shouldn't
- Be a bystander when someone is being bullied
- Break laws
- Bully others
- Cheat
- Develop eating habits that lead to disorders
- Disrespect others
- Drink alcohol
- Drop out of school
- Engage in an intimate relationship before you are ready
- Harm an animal
- Have unprotected sex
- Hurt any person, verbally or physically
- Join a questionable group of people/gang
- Lie
- Smoke
- Use drugs
- Vandalize

Whole Person Associates is the leading publisher of training resources for professionals who empower people to create and maintain healthy lifestyles. Our creative resources will help you work effectively with your clients in the areas of stress management, wellness promotion, mental health and life skills.

Please visit us at our web site: **WholePerson.com**. You can check out our entire line of products, place an order, request our print catalog, and sign up for our monthly special notifications.

Whole Person Associates

800-247-6789